Grief's L

and

other poems

Lisa Albright Ratnavira

illustrations by Gamini Ratnavira

GARDEN OAK PRESS

Garden Oak Press
1953 Huffstatler St., Suite A
Rainbow, CA 92028
760 728-2088
gardenoakpress.com
gardenoakpress@gmail.com

First published by Garden Oak Press on July 1, 2017

ISBN-13:   978-1548051136

ISBN-10:   1548051136

Printed in the United States of America

To the daughter of my heart, **Natalie Ann**, who passed away on June 23, 2012 from an atrial venous malformation.

May her spirit continue to dance with ours as she ventures into dreams we cannot yet imagine. I know we will each find one another again in order to continue this sacred pact of love for nature, for art, for one another.

Natalie was a Wildlife Conservation and Ecology Major at the University of Reno, as well as the striker for its soccer team.

Scholarships in her name are distributed annually to allow future students of flora and fauna and conservation, to continue her passion.

CONTENTS

Grief's Labyrinth

Other Poems

Grief's Labyrinth

Inspired by
Octavio Paz

Afterword by **Robert Louis Chianese**

GARDEN OAK PRESS
Rainbow, California

Labyrinth

Her first headache, a labyrinth of questions.
We turn into the 3rd floor CCU waiting room.
Friends float in with sandwiches, coffee, tea.
They twist in tight plastic chairs.
Prayers, kind messages, get lost in the blast
of the intercom, squeak of gurneys moving
our daughter into rooms we can't find.
Surgeries. She is attached to machines with
wires and chords, coiled and twisted like snakes.
Medicines cloud and close her eyes. They place
her scalp within her abdomen to keep her scalp alive.
They hope to reattach her scalp to her skull
when her brain swelling reduces.

Our own dark corridors, the snarls and twists of what ifs.
We watch the brain pressure numbers,
greet our friends, so many friends their faces
keep changing. We act like politicians or
royalty and they wait for our answers.
The neurosurgeon's strong steps echo
in the corridors. Fluorescent lights brighten.
He says with a smile, "Optimistic."
The only outcome we'll allow is a win.

After three surgeries, the doctor's words
echo and boom through the maze
of empty hallways. There has been a massive
assault to all four regions of our daughter's brain.
No language, no movement, no capacity
to communicate, eat, to tell us
what she feels, needs.
The doctor who taught us to hope,
now grieves for us.
The labyrinth, the hospital's hallways,
turn black. We know the choice
our family must make.

We allow life support to end.

Family surrounds her, making peace, saying regrets.
Promises bathe her. She battles on, morphine
and Ativan for her pain.

Three brothers at her bedside. Thanking her,
loving her, touching her. That trickster,
the labyrinth turns again.
We follow, but only Natalie finds the exit.

The labyrinth now our tears,
our to-do lists, our what ifs that echo down
one corridor, our if onlys chasing us down
the next. Above our maze, a hummingbird
hovers, a pair of dragonflies glide across
a creek where she and her younger brothers
once caught water striders.

The labyrinth takes over our home, settles in our room.
The oven and fridge beep open. We picture her wide smile
when she smelled homemade brownies, Snicker Doodles, roast.
Her animals search for her. Her parents
pine for her, we sob while we hang
her paintings, her photos. We eke out
thank you notes to the village that loved
our daughter.

The longest curve, the final twist, leaves
us alone at our dining table, where we see
her empty chair, or even at restaurants where we
still ask for six. (Our hostess sees only five.)
Our inside joke, the joke she is not here
to catch.

"So unfair," we say, "taking one so precious
to us." We stomp up stairways, kick walls.
We slump exhausted in chairs and couches
where she used to sit. We know our nightmare
is real.

continued

3

The ashes we bury are our daughter's.
We wail and weep at the labyrinth's wall.
We beg the labyrinth to set us free, to allow
us passage.

And the only exit is marked *impermanence*.
Outside the labyrinth, the meadow blooms
with sweet peas. A gray fox stops for a second,
blinks and continues.

We cover our eyes then look deeply into one
another's eyes.
And know we will begin to dream once more
with our eyes closed.

What Not to Say
to a Mother Who Has Lost Her Child?

1. At least you have other children. . .

2. How are you?

3. Was she saved?

4. You can imagine her in heaven.

5. Was that why she was gay?
     (The cerebral hematoma in her left temporal lobe)

6. I miss your laugh.

7. When do you think you can come back
     . . .to work, to tennis, to _____ .

9. Time heals. . .

10. I have a friend who had an AVM and woke up from her coma just fine.

What to Say or Do

bring wine   bring food
bring your tears but not so many i have to comfort you
bring your favorite photos, memories, quotes
bring a blanket   plan on staying
bring paper towels
or household items so we don't have to go to the market
and answer endless questions
bring a plant   bring a tree
bring a wind chime
bring a hummingbird feeder
bring a pen to help write thank you notes
bring a laptop to help write lists, obits, programs
bring thick skin so we can swear
                  and not worry we have lost you too
bring a book to stay   maybe we can sleep if someone is here
bring a candle or tea light or lamp
bring a memory
bring a CD with chosen songs
bring a hug
     and don't be afraid if we hold you too long or not at all
bring a card that says a favorite meal shared
     or memory together
     or has a note of i don't know what the heck to say
                  but i wish i did
bring money
the overwhelming reality of funeral and medical costs
                is beyond fathomable
bring patience
the healing is in the telling of the story
           we may repeat ourselves for years
bring awareness
     the rest of our life will be before
          our daughter died and after we lost her. . .

bring a shovel   we will want to plant a garden
bring a cool rock
bring your kindness
calls that say I am thinking of you,
      there are no words for your loss,
         just know I am here thinking of you
every day. . .
bring anything that symbolizes who she was to you
                    or who we are to you
we can't feel anything right now
    so know when we remember your visit
      we will feel all of it. . .just not now

Lisa

If (I)

   We could talk for one more hour
If
   I could go to one more of your animal shows
If
   We could laugh together once more
If
   I could hold you one last time
If
   I could tell you once more how your beautiful smile
                                lit up our home
If
   I could tell you once more how your appetite
               made me want to bake and cook and create
If
   I could touch you once more and share with you
                      how beautiful you are
If
   I could travel to Sri Lanka with you one more time
If
   I could complete all your albums and turn each page
       reliving our future vacations   your soccer game
               our holidays together
If
   I could take you to one more Pride
If
   I had one more chance to cherish you. . .

If (II)

If you are running in a meadow with a fox, butterflies
                                    and ladybugs
lion-headed rabbits and hummingbirds
If your smile is the sparkle in the next rainbow
If your loving heart continues in each friendship
                            you gave your spirit to
If every animal you rescued is there beside you
If every soccer ball you kicked arcs through
                                canyons that echo
If you are full, complete, at peace,
                    with loved ones who adore you
If I can learn to live without you
the daughter of my heart
I will not stop believing
all of this is there for you
and that one day
your loving arms will welcome me once more

Hiccups

When my first baby
hiccupped inside me
for minutes on end
I felt the movement.
I knew I could do nothing
to help.
When my only daughter, at age 22
on a ventilator, in a coma
would hiccup
for seven straight minutes
I remembered how her Daddy
told her to breathe in and out
s l o w l y through her nose.
She hated her hiccups.
At the hospital when we watched her
slip away from all of us
we knew
she would never
struggle with hiccups again.

Saying Goodbye –
Her Birth Mother and I

Softly I kissed her hand
as the last of her breath
rattled from her chest
midwifing this journey as I have for another once before.
Her birth mother pronounced her dead at 12:56 p.m.
and I wept as I witnessed her prepare
her only child's body
yet as I left the room
I heard her whisper to Nat,
      "What is between us is behind us, go to the light"
and I knew Nat would find rainbows.

Life on Life's Terms

is overrated
I miss my pink glasses
my effervescent optimism
This new anger, apathy
is not welcome
I dislike impermanence
fluidity
motion
I ache for her laugh   her smile
her ability to take risks
her color-coded closets
the toucans she painted for her father
Please remake this
Embed her life into my own
as a seahorse carries its young

The Bonsai Gardener

I watch him train
the trees to shape the design
he pictures
He coils and wraps the wire
from trunk to branch
executes each angle
chooses some beloved foliage
to stay and removes
the unwanted leaves
each choice with intention
like a spider's web
catching light and enhancing beauty
courting death
If only I were so willing to accept
The Master of Garden's sheers
to fancy
any other outcome
except the one
that removed
our most exquisite foliage

It's Been Three Months

since you've been gone
There is no reason for me to carry on
I look at every butterfly, hummingbird and flower
and lose all the meaning   all the power
I want nothing more than to laugh with you
to roll our eyes
paint our nails
bake for the boys
and cry   two grown women together
Now I navigate alone
territory far too familiar
lonely as a queen bee
I miss my girl
I miss your laugh
your endless *To Do* list
your llama llama red pajamas
come back to me in dreams
in light in any form

She Left Me With

working all day in my classroom
that has her spirit everywhere
Her presentation
of the wallaby, the python, the alligator
the hedgehog, the ferret and the Fennec fox
Her photos on my computer
I sob as I look at the sunflowers bowed seed-laden heads
remembering the time she was rushed
to the hospital, their blooms were a sign
she would be okay
I rip them out of their garden beds
with a fury that even I did not know
was within me
I make it   somehow   mercifully   through the day
pull in weary to my driveway
and my neighbor, Marilyn, greets me:
"Lisa, life is cruel, here are some tomatoes"
They grow in her garden
from the rotten tomatoes she buried last summer.
Marilyn survived a mother who left her at age seven
and danced back in when Marilyn was 17
Marilyn cared for her husband for decades after his stroke
I slice the tomatoes over Portuguese beans,
the recipe my Nana Ann gave me
Ann buried every one of her four sons and her daughter Mary
My daughter left me with so many gifts:
to love without abandon or apology,
the way she loved wallabies, sunflowers, and foxes,
juicy women, fresh tomatoes and Portuguese beans
This labyrinth of grief winds me back to her

Daily Chores

The laundry on the lines reveals
crisp whites enhanced with robin blue powder
washed with melodious song in the nearby streams
over rocks more ancient than this rich heritage
Saris and sarongs and linens
subjected to afternoon tropical rains
wrung out
hung once more
hanging in the symbolic colors of
Buddhist prayer flags
Whites for enlightenment, yellow for the wind, orange as fire,
red for power
and blues for the water they are washed with
The clothes on the line hang
announce the joy of a family within

Note: At just about the six month mark, we flew back to Sri Lanka to honor our daughter in the Ratnavira family Buddhist Temple and to give some donations in her name: to build a bridge for the school children, a venom program's research fund, a rainforest program and a child at Prithipura Infant Home named Nethmi, who the family, including Natalie, had supported since the Sri Lankan tsunami in 2004.

Nethmi

After loving you for five-and-a-half years
I discover you are
a little girl   not a boy after all
Your shorn hair was to prevent bed bugs
Your boy-like outfits were all they had
Mute, you could not voice your disapproval
We walk and stomp and play
You smile from deep within
My fears transform to joy
The white butterfly lands
on the bougainvillea as you grasp my hand
and lead me down your lane
I imagine a different world for us
free to paint and sign and swim
for your hair to grow
for me to braid it and
adorn it with butterflies
I imagine the clothes I would
buy for you   my little waif
I imagine guiding you
and seeking all that I might provide
for you
You have awakened
the dormant seeker
within
There is a purpose beyond us
our lives intertwine
I navigate with
kindness, openness
to enhance your life
but it is my duty
to not entangle you
in my grief

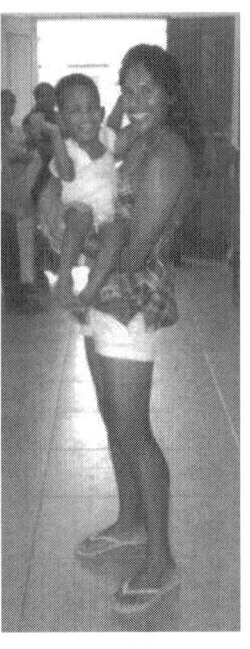

A Wish for the New Year

May all living beings
    be well and happy
May they be healthy
    and free from disease
May they be free from
    mental and physical suffering
May they lead a life
    rich with tolerance
        compassion and patience
May they experience
    good will, friendliness and joy
May they smile at death
    aware of the absence
    of a lasting and unchanging soul
        resolving to live a noble life
            in honor of all departed loved ones

January 1, 2013
Sri Lanka

Ladybug, Ladybug, Fly Away

eggs, larvae, pupae,
ladybug, ladybug fly away
your house is on fire
your children aren't safe.
Red and black are warning colors
I'm obsessed with them.
I decorate my car and my classrooms with ladybugs.
My gardens are rich with them.
What is this life awakening within me?
A realization that my daughter Natalie
has transformed
she is free
and yet, I'm here
still hovering with
aphids and marigolds.

Learning to Release

I hold Vanessa's hand
I show up
I give her two matching charm bracelet beads
knowing when I meet her mom
one will be for her
and one to keep
I bring purple and pink flowering verbenas
and the strength bracelet she gave to me last summer
I am confidant
I am strong
I have been here before
exactly here when I said good bye to Addie

I placed an orchid for Addie and my great granddad earlier
I ask to be introduced to her 46 year-old mom
who has joined my 22 year-old daughter
I hold Vanessa's hand   my teacher in her mid 20's
I stand beside her at 44
I tell her to place a bead inside her mom's coffin
I place the flowers near the burial site
I wait and watch
She reminds me of a giraffe toy I played with when I was small
fascinated that when I pushed the bottom
the strings would loosen
and the giraffe would crumble in a heap
when I released it, the strings would tighten
and it would stand upright once again
I see Vanessa crumbling
I have been here before
still crumbling
I ask questions like why not me and Nat
or Vanessa and her mom?
Why separate two sets of love for no reason?
Who is pushing the bottoms
and forgetting to release us?

Why the hell do I know exactly what to do
at this funeral
just 10 months after I forgot to bring something
to include in my daughter's ashes
just 10 months after not knowing what to wear, what to say
after not being able to remember who was there?
Now I walk away after *Amazing Grace*
remembering how we sang
Amazing Grace as we disconnected Nat's life support
I remember when I used to want that song sung for me
now I am considering something different
something like, *Raise Your Glass* by Pink
or
Have you ever thrown a handful of glitter in the air?
I envy the dead
I rage at the grief left in the wake
I crumple at the hands of the one
wielding this toy

"Hey, Nat"

I fell to my knees
looking up at Beau's nearly six-foot stature.
"What's wrong Mom?"
"I thought you were saying hi to your sister."
I heard the way your voice rose
when you greeted your sister in the morning
Your secret ninja twin,
Brooks, her baby brother wakes.
Now 17, 6' 1" and filled with all that is yet to be a man
I see them laughing, dancing together
riding go carts and getting matching scars.
I yearn for her, my only daughter,
the only female ally in our clan
and I serve the meal to her brothers and her Dad
and I want her here, pouring the waters, rolling her eyes at me
at the silly things they say.
I remember one of her confessions:
"I am so afraid one of my lovers,
will fall for my baby brother he is so gorgeous,
so sculpted how can I compete with that?"
I laughed as I gazed at her perfectly sculpted body
and the smile that lit up our home,
that she could ever worry about being left.

The Invitation

to UNReno's alumni game arrived.
She remembers her puma stance, her karate style kicks,
her ninja rolls, when Coach Raffi called her Kwanzaa.
She remembers when she wore
Nat's 12-year-old soccer photo badge on her vest
and cheered for her daughter in the stands.
She remembers Nat in her *nattitude* braids and braces
and Coach Jaime, her UNR coach, proudly wore
the same soccer badge much to Nat's embarrassment.
She misses watching Nat on the field, striking the winning goal.
She prays she is reaching a far greater goal in a different field.
She hopes Nat knows she is loved,
she is missed, her family is trying to carry on
her dream of research in Sri Lanka
the best we can.
She knows she won't attend this game
but hopes Nat throws a rainbow over the field at half time
just for kicks.

Paper Chains

Lisa and Rae used paper chains, one link a day
to anticipate the next celebration
Lisa calls with this week's paper chain
asks Rae about the recent meeting of Matt's family
Rae says they liked one another and it went well
Lisa knows Rae knocked them out
with her strawberry tresses and beauty
She tells Rae about the weekend   Good Friday with Heidi
She and Heidi had a paper chain
for a date for pedicures and shopping
their first friendship date since Natalie's death
pedicures and shopping for the first time in months
Lisa sat waiting for Heidi and a stranger sat beside her,
Lisa observes a mother and her daughters arrive
choosing their nail polish colors
"She'll be buying pedicures for 80 years," the stranger comments
Lisa retorts: "I can't even hear this.
I just lost my daughter this summer"
Furious that there are not 80 more manicures for her to buy
she storms out the door   Later
Rae listens to her roommate in Oregon
so excited about her new ramp, her new bus route,
her newfound freedom
and then receives her late night call after Easter Sunday
Her friend's urine collecting jar toppled
Her grip was not strong enough
Got on her cell phone charger and lit the wall on fire
Her neighbors rushed in to save her on Easter Sunday
Rae listens to these two dearer than sisters
She knows her news of newfound love
of finding her person   of loving each other and their families
should she share this joy or
will it remind them of all they have lost

Her guilt bounces knowing had fate taken a different turn
this could be her own Mom and Nat sharing paper chains
She could be the one in a wheelchair
She listens on the phone
penning Matthew, Matthew, Matthew
Torn chains litter her bedroom floor

Standing Here 2

Standing in the creek my daughter played in
we caught water striders
in mayonnaise jars
She played sword fights
with bamboo reeds
with her little brothers here
I stand with the echoes of their laughter
here
rocks spilling out of my apron
the white quartz of Frost's promises
lying to me
The robin overhead sings
I hear, "Your life is pure vanity"
She was the one meant to be standing here
My life so empty of her passions for animals, rainbows,
soccer, the elderly, the special needs some children bring
her smile capable of lighting up our home
our lives
her gentleness so calming so grateful
her sadness so deep
I stand here empty
throwing the smooth granite stones from my pockets
I curse Emily, I curse Virginia
hating the words that still tumble forth
Holding me here
the ripples remind me of the love I have for our sons,
my husband, the paintings he is yet to create
that I so desperately want to see
the possibilities of granddaughters one day
The hope of those damn poets
words swimming within me
holding me here
Standing here in the rock-strewn creek bed
I grab hold
I climb out

Metta Sutta

Feeling inspired, watching Gam paint, we discuss the Jataka stories
and Metta Sutta or loving kindness.
Here's my take on the Metta Sutta:

May all loving beings
seek the path to peace
becoming grounded, not chasing status
Born or yet to be born
may all beings be happy in themselves
releasing anger   embracing loving kindness
like a parent with her own child
protecting that child with her own life
This infinite love we give to one another
and honor our wise elders who walked these paths before us
May all beings everywhere
laugh with their entire soul
freed from doubts and permanency

Entering the Holidays

For those of us who have lost a child, attending events and milestones are especially difficult questions about how many children do you have? Are your children coming home this year? Although kindly meant, these questions are like blows to an already crippling grief.

Put on the war makeup
Separate each black lash
perfectly coated in perspective
Smile with painted lips
Lubricate the lies
Enjoy the enemy
Powder painted cheeks
Embellish false joy
Place each sculpted leg in silk stockings
holding in the survivors flight tendency
Adorn jewelry for purposes of show
not sweet emotion
Tall shoes projecting slender images
Illusions of height to match
The illusion of family
Adorned with armor
to fight emotional arrows
Step with the security
that the hours will pass by
excruciatingly slow
and then you can exhale
the toxic gathering
and breathe deeply
the green trees, the sunshine
the love of souls
wrapped tightly around your heart
and return to the
sanctuary of peace
you have created within

Snicker Doodles

So I am trying so hard to find normal again
I invite Ellie, my youngest son Brooks' girlfriend,
to bake Snicker Doodles with me and we are having a great time
Finally the dough is prepared and I invite her to try it:
"I know some people are freaks about the eggs and salmonella
but none of my kids ever died"
I break   I stop   I am spiraling   I don't have a save here
She pops the cookie dough in her mouth
and says, "Of salmonella – it's okay
none of them died from your cookie dough, Lis."

"Delicious"   She sways away with knowing hips
She shares these wounds
Her mom died eight years ago
She knows what loss feels like
how sometimes in the middle of joy,
thanks to a medical abnormality
you are plummeted into sorrow without warning
She has tasted this before
She is the perfect girl to make Snicker Doodles with

Heller's Bend, My Sanctuary

I watch
light pouring through clouds
the creek rushing
waters caressing rocks
mosses and lichens and mushrooms dancing between rye grasses
green as Ireland
Brooke's bench, recalling the fairies we used to hang above.
Now I hang them in the tree above Nat's memorial stone.
Quail tracks lost into the trail
coyote scat. I hear the children singing.
It starts with an S and ends with a T
comes out of you, comes out of me
laughter echoes in my memories.
A heart carved deeply in the towering oak,
dew drops on oak and sage leaves
like diamonds formed from fairy dust.
Rocks strewn with leaves oak saplings and ferns.

I listen
to the creek's water rushing to the San Luis Rey River
titmouse towhee chirping above
a hummingbird whirring and singing *a capella*
branches cracking.
I hear the echoes of my children playing, laughing
gathering flowers together these past 20 years.

I smell
the intoxicating rain pure and clean
the oxygen embracing my lungs.
Sage to purify my grief.
Lichens and mosses on stone wrap me in their beauty
and lose me in their musty strength.

I absorb
this stoic beauty in my grieving empty womb.
I welcome this quiet beauty
and photograph this creek
where I come to find a God
I can make peace with
the same God who gifted me these beautiful children
embracing me with their love, their laughter, their racing feet
and stole my daughter before her children could walk with me
here
pour their angst and heartache out to me on these paths
as she did
but gave her to me just the same
gifted me her smile, her love, her faith in nature.

I pray.

Letter from a Friend Regarding Grief

I do have some suggestions – I will write some here:

First of all, take very good care of yourself – get plenty of rest, eat regularly, get a massage every week. Losing a member of your immediate family is a huge adjustment to make, and you want to help your physiology as well as your emotions and spirit. So don't skimp on the basics of living – eating, sleeping, drinking, etc.

Be really gentle with yourself. Buy yourself some flowers, or listen to music, or read poems, or do all three.

Don't try to pretend you are ok. Sometimes you will be fine, and other times you will feel very fragile. It comes and goes like that.

Forgive people who say tactless things. There are always a few clueless people. Don't let it get to you. They really don't know any better.

Figure out what works for you – getting away from people or being with them, or a mix. And figure out with whom. Distraction (a movie, or whatever) is fine. You want to "dose" yourself – in the sense of giving yourself a break every day from the hugeness of what has happened. You go to the movie, or hang out with people – people who don't know what happened – and this gives your heart a little rest from the hurt. And then you're able to feel it again.

The work that Elizabeth Kubler-Ross did on grief was ground-breaking, but later it was discovered that things don't move in a linear way (first shock, then denial, then guilt, anger, bargaining, and acceptance).

There is an online grief support (www.hellogrief.org). You can find other survivors who are in a similar place, but log off when it is too much to feel.

You will feel more like a spiral of feelings – some return, some wane, it just happens as it happens. . .but eventually I promise your heart will heal and eventually it won't seem like it happened just yesterday. Eventually your heart will feel whole again, and you will feel much more love than grief.

One more thing. Go to a health food store and get some *Rescue Remedy* – it's a flower essence for shock and trauma and put a few drops in your water and sip it throughout the day. It will help.

Oops – very important. Think of all the good memories of your loved one. Send them love. They didn't go far. They are close to you and feel your love, and you can feel theirs. Not that much has actually changed. They just don't have a body anymore. Otherwise, you still have a relationship, and are close and always will be.

The Mobile

A delicate balance
rotates, dances
Music soothing and comforting
sustains us
We watch mesmerized
as the intricate connectedness suspends
individual pieces tied together
shifting, changing connecting
until the purple star
is cut away
The entire mobile shifts
off kilter
Some tie off together
too heavy to float
Some spiral alone, spinning
The music too
skips and hits
long silences
Where does one begin
to balance
re-string, replenish
or does
the disbanded mobile
disappear in a box
labeled, *Needs repair*

Message from a Sedona Healer at the Hummingbird Festival

Hello Lisa and Gamini,

I trust you had a safe journey home!

It was such a pleasure to meet you both and I am so glad you joined us at the festival.

Meeting you two was a highlight of the festival for me!

Below is the message I received from Natalie. Thank you for receiving it so openly. This does not happen often for me, yet on occasion, there is someone who has an important message and somehow they know that I will be open to receive it and pass it on.

As I sat quietly in the dark auditorium listening to Jacques's lecture, a gentle spirit tapped me on the shoulder and asked if I would convey a message. That gentle spirit was Natalie.

She wanted me to tell Lisa, "I loved you as much as I love my Dad. Thank you for taking care of my kitties. My heart sings when I see you and Dad at the event this weekend. I am free. There are so many creatures here! I am learning so much and I am with the animals. *All* the animals are here, prehistoric, extinct, *all* the animals."

I asked Natalie if there was any message she wanted me to take to her Dad. She replied, "No, that is not necessary, he knows all of this. I am a part of him."

Many Blessings to you both and I hope our paths cross again soon,

Jackie

Note: When I walked a labyrinth here in Sedona, there was a Zen garden, a dragonfly, a butterfly, a sunflower, rocks and minerals, and I knew this journey would leave me open to the message above.

Women Face Dying with Familiarity

We have been dying little deaths since the beginning
First our eggs
Then in giving birth
noting a window where it would be so easy to leave
and yet having so many reasons to stay, we resurface
In the arms of a skilled lover we experience little deaths
and re-emerge stronger and more vital than before
Women die a bit every month curled over   cramping
facing the hurricane of emotions that takes over our bodies
In our children, we die for them with each tear, every heartache
We face life as a cruel task master and oblige our chores
our roles with a certainty of death to release us
from the torture our bodies at times bestow upon us
Women and death are like the cycles in a garden we are sown,
we sow, we reap, we diminish, unlike our male counterparts
 facing a life of virility often into eight decades
They lose a bit of testosterone in the middle years
but seem to age with grace, become more distinguished
not lugging kangaroo pouches where babies once formed
or breasts now sagging after they were once filled
with the milk that nourished others, proving to ourselves
our bodies are miracles, after hating them
during our teen years, making peace
with the roadmaps of wrinkles and scars
that claim us, mother above all
But when a mother buries her own child
when she watches that child exhale for the last time
she too breathes out begging
for the gods to allow her to trade places
asking how long 'til the children can be whole once again
inside her, beside her
and she breathes knowing death is universally cruel
and not kind for many breaths to come
She knows the way a mama bird knows
when her nestling takes flight too near a scrub jay
that her heart will forever be missing that love
that oneness of spirit

And yet, for the babies to return to, for the babies not yet met
for the mothers who have never known childbirth
she continues, she loves, she rages, she bakes, she laughs
and she cries for the same reasons
Her labyrinth of life cycles, much like Daedalus
creating the original Labyrinth for King Minos,
she loves her job so well she can barely escape it
searching for a way out and a way in simultaneously
A job well done is a job left locked inside the labyrinth
The release is up to a captor she has not yet met
the voice her own.

I Carry Death Within Me

like a still born child
inside my grieving womb
reminding me with each breath,
labored, worn,
my life should have been
shed for hers
so she could feel the love
of a baby's heartbeat
a kick inside of her
the hiccups within her womb,
not robbed of all of this
emptying what remains of me for them.

The Daughters I Know

a response to *The Mothers I Know*, by PENNY PERRY

The daughters I know
could all be married now
the young
champagne
vows, rings
promises
of their own.

The daughters I know
could have graduated
could be with child.

Margaret is getting married in July.
Hannah is finishing her teaching program.
Rae is in her MFA.
Here at work, Nat's ex sent tulips to her girlfriend
on Valentine's Day
in memory of their shared love for our Valentine's girl
and their newly pledged love for one another.

The daughters I know
could have walked the aisle
wombs fertile
baby showers attended.

I trace my daughter's name
in labrydite:
     NATALIE ANN RATNAVIRA
     FEB. 14, 1990 – JUNE 23, 2012.

It Was Always Anybody's Game

title suggested by RAE ROSE

I.

Am I less than you
with only three sons
to call my own?
When I had four
to share with you
when Saturdays
did not include placing flowers
on my only daughter's gravestone
was I your equal?
Does my grief
shatter your
possibilities?
Does my brokenness
mirror your
own inadequacies?
My womb delivered
two healthy sons,
my heart brought me
two more children to love.
The inadequacy
of a single artery
leaves me
longing for the
mother-daughter tennis tournament
we can no longer play.
We would have won.
We were that good
together.
Am I no longer
worthy of your
attention now
that as a mother
I have failed?

II.

After suffering the greatest loss
a heart can bear,
now how do your "caught her sneaking out,
with a tattoo, a forbidden lover, dropping out of school"
stories compare?

Am I less than you
or did fate deliver me
a blow that left me so shattered
and yet still here,
still baking for my sons,
making sweet love to my husband,
remembering to call my closest friends?

Am I less than you?
My shame buries me.
My loss is a weight,
too great to bear alone
and, yes, my weight gain
reflects my grief.
Try putting down your
survivor's guilt
and showing up,
try a card, a call
a gesture.
It's not contagious.

A Garden Full (II)

Addie and *Agnes*, born before 1910, gave us jade and pink ladies,
Dr. Johanek and Dr. Bliss – irises, and aloes.
Geraniums and honeysuckle, a wedding gift
                                        from Kate & Bill in 2002.
Jesse and Rae: calla lilies and moonflowers.

Grammy gifted ginger from her trip to Hawaii.
Dad tilled the land while I was in labor so the flowers
that arrived after my second son's birth in 1995 would thrive,
each of us sharing hours of labor, ending in breathtaking beauty.
Banana trees, resurrections ferns and Australian parakeets
                                        given by Richard
along with a soul that grieves with ours, side by side.
Sugar cane from *Ed.*
Ice cream bean trees and passion fruit given by Mary and Ben.

Nanny planted impatients and bougainvillea
to celebrate the life of her third grandson.
Nancy nursed willow saplings that entice swallowtails,
their eggs and larvae, much to our children's delight.
Greg lavished us with kalanchos, orchids, succulents,
staghorns and 100-year old bonsais.
Three Chinese flame trees created a forest to share with others.
Noriega granted us a Guava tree.
The Beran's orchids and bulbs to share as we have shared
our children with one another for two decades.

The Adachi's adorned our koi ponds with water lilies.
Lynette brought bromeliads. Don in Bali, Daturas,
a visit from *Dennis*, a dwarf aloe and turtle.
Epiphyllums awaken in a hot pink starburst for just one day.
Walt gifted rare Panamanian orchids
with a story and painting from each one.
Linda T. sent us a bo tree, a peacock fern
and a Buddha's hand from Florida.
Linda B. arrived with a 25-year-old cattalaya,
the Costa Rican national flower, for our gallery's opening.

Juls left her beloved plumerias in our care
as her family left to Virginia. I send her photos of their blooms.
Heidi and Hank lavish us with African violets
and the special pots that contain them in our kitchen.
Friends bring cuttings and bulbs for dinner gifts,
or leave them unexpectedly at our door
knowing they will be cherished, nurtured back to life.
Great Aunt Jo in her 90's, the most devout Catholic in my life,
gifted us a gardenia bonsai when the grief of our only daughter
ripped open our souls

Sweet pea seeds, collected throughout California,
all blooming the fragrance of memories gathered,
our children picking them and discovering striations
and newfound colors with unabated joy.
I see *Nat* and Beau and Brooks in each bloom.

Our string of hearts last propagated by our daughter, *Natalie*,
who now hovers with the dragonflies,
occasionally caught in a spiders web,
so her Daddy can still get her out of sticky situations
 is always near to this momentary veil we call life

Her memory and fairy gardens, built and honored
by her family, each brother Neil, Beau and Brooks
adding a special rock from their journeys.
We tend to our daughter's memory the way parents
awaiting their newborn decorate the nursery,
planting and watering and revisiting
her laugh, her appetite, her love for us
and these beautiful gardens.

The last decades, riddled with the highs and lows
of lives lived, carry on in our garden.
Many friends remain. *Some loved ones have moved on.*
We pay our respects to each
as we weed and fertilize and nurture
this land we are growing on.

Planting Daffodils

Kate gives me daffodil bulbs
for my birthday.
"Gophers hate them!" she beams
as her daughter Rae
is mesmerized with Nat's fairy garden.

I receive them and know
exactly where they'll go,
next to Nat's memorial garden:
a purple heart-shaped stone
laden with momentos from around the world –
lava from Mt Fuji from Beau,
a slice of granite and quartz from Brook's 16th birthday
Yosemite hiking trip the brothers took with Joe.
Near Nat's paper narcissus bulbs lies a rock
from Kelley after her pilgrimage to India.
A Buddhist oil lamp from the temples of Sri Lanka, too.
I place the bulbs in the earth –
my 45th year, she was given only 22 –
I cover them gently
like the way Kate brought me lentil soup,
listened to my poems over and over again,
exploring the why's
the absence
the underlying guilt:
"It should have been me."
She gives me hope in a bulb without predators.
She knows my sweet peas are lost
in my memories of Nat and yet I sow them still.
She knows my grief.
Our parallels run deeper than the soil.
I tuck these sweet daffodils in.
She recounts my life in numbers
and flowers and words
lovingly written between us.

I receive them
I sow them.
I may pick them
for an Ikebana arrangement
and bring them back to her.
Either way,
daughters and bulbs
and a friendship over 20 years
are impermanent in nature
and yet live on
in the hands we embrace,
in the words we write,
in the laugh lines we share.
Kate has given me bulbs
pregnant with possibilities.

She Practiced

loving kindness
generosity
compassion for animals
She smiled
in a way that broke your heart wide open
She laughed bent over
gasping for joy
She danced
as if her very bones were fluid
She left this world as a lotus flower
giving even what remained to others
selfless
Now she hovers
in the spirits of dragonflies
sending ripples of love
in every still pond

And Yet

As a gossamer floret
I danced into my destiny
earnestly blooming with sunshine
and carrying my grandmother's identity, too.
My yellow petals fell away one by one
as I transformed
into a full moon of alabaster wishes
leaving me heady with possibilities.
I released each floret with care
except for one sole pappus.
She took flight ahead of the others.
These wishes left me changed
less than the dream-filled golden dandelion
the fertile white gossamer blow ball.
Bent in prayer like a monk's shaven head
I leave this field almost invisible, and yet
my dreams remain.

Scattering Sweet Peas

She searches patiently
Dark tresses dancing
in the scented breeze
past the thousands of maroon-tinted sweet peas
intoxicating and beautiful
for the one striated with lavender, dusted with pink
She walks gently between their climbing vines
easing a poppy seed pod open
spreading hundreds of babies for next spring
She labors for the one spectacular blossom
erupting in smiles
she brings in the
irresistible bouquet
filling our kitchen with the aroma
of such warmth, sun kissed petals
exquisite in our home

Years later I am left searching
alone , discovering
lavender, baby pink striations
I pick the maroon, the common
leaving the one-in-a-million
to recreate her smile in my garden
in my every breath
I keep her sweetness here
so that in her absence
we are not divided

AFTERWARD

Grief's Labyrinth: The Progress of Mourning

by ROBERT LOUIS CHIANESE

This remarkable collection of poems by LISA ALBRIGHT RATNAVIRA traces the stages of mourning by the poet for her lost daughter who died of an atrial venous malformation at the tender age of 22. This malady may serve as the source of the metaphoric title of the collection, which includes delicate art works by her artist husband. The title page shows a labyrinth with crossed dividing lines, as if to represent the misconnections between the arteries and veins that took Natalie Ann's life.

There are other such labyrinths through the poem: hospital corridors, paper chains, but most importantly the labyrinth of grief that traps and overtakes the poet/mother even as she finds temporary relief in vivid memories, extensive travels, and family time when Natalie was alive. Besides the 36 poems in the title section there are two other sections with poems of different times.

Poetic art that mourns the loss of someone has a long tradition in western art. In the form called the elegy, the poet mourns some famous figure, such as Whitman mourning the loss of Abraham Lincoln in *When Lilacs Last in the Dooryard Bloom'd,* or Shelley mourning the untimely death of Keats in *Adonais.* The convention usually involves a distance between the elegist and the dead person. But in *In Memoriam,* Tennyson mourns his friend Arthur Hallam, also dead at 22, and the elegy becomes personal, introspective and private and so even more encumbered by anguish, which must be somehow relieved for the elegaic process or action to be complete. This is intensified in mother Lisa trying to come to grips with daughter Natalie's passing.

The formal design of the elegy actually helps one work through personal loss. In order to reconcile oneself to the death, a simple but difficult formula must be worked out: "She is dead / She is Not Dead" is the abstract pattern. To get from one statement to the other requires a redefinition of both life and death, some transcendent moment of realizing the person is not actually dead, and a celebration of life in the midst of loss. This emotional and mental process usually employs formal language and elevated diction. This Ratnavira accomplishes, despite frequent relapses into doubt, anger and despair, but with the powerful ability to move between these contrary states with a simple, direct, often colloquial language that expresses both.

The title poem is the longest and the most graphic about the medical details and the fretting over the words of hope, then no hope that the doctor utters so that the hospital is a kind of trap:

> The labyrinth, the hospital's hallways,
> turn black. We know the choice
> our family must make.
> We allow life support to end.

But even in this first poem with its list of various labyrinths – questions, tears, what ifs, an actual maze by creekside, the home and its physical prompts of memory, the poet announces the elegiac process:

> And the only exit is marked "impermanence."
> Outside the labyrinth the meadow blooms
> with sweet peas. A gray fox stops for a second,
> blinks and continues.

Only acceptance of "impermanence" can lead out of the maze of pain, here to a meadow with a tangle of sweet peas and a passing fox. The world of ordinary process goes on, with a second key metaphor announced almost prematurely – the blooms of sweet pea flowers, signaling the acceptance of death and impermanence that the poet will fully arrive at in later poems.

There is a formality to the language in most of this, but short lines and simple vocabulary blend in a colloquial sound. The listing of the Ifs the poet wishes she had in *If (I)* and *If (II)* is so direct and ordinary we seem to be overhearing her inner prayer of negotiation with life itself, almost a promise to herself what she would do to have her daughter back. But in *Hiccups*, the familiar comic action of a baby becomes tragic as Natalie hiccups "for seven straight minutes" in a coma, so that a soothing recollection of childhood turns harsh and brutal and unrelieved. These motherly reflections recur throughout the poems, venting grief and anguish, but not without a partial resolution – here the somewhat merciful recognition that she will not hiccup again. The colloquial can serve tragedy.

In *Daily Chores*, she gets closer to acceptance even as the locale turns to the many exotic places where the family has traveled. In doing laundry, this time presumably in Sri Lanka, the poet sees signs of renewal:

> Saris and sarongs and linens
> subjected to afternoon tropical rains
> wrung out
> hung once more
> hanging in the symbolic colors of
> Buddhist prayer flags
> Whites for enlightenment. . .

The middle lines, "wrung out/hung once more," could spark a new bout of grief, but here the colorful clothes provide comfort and "announce the joy of a family within." This is reinforced by the realization that like a ladybug, Natalie "has transformed/ she is free, " yet there is no full rejoicing since the poet is not free, nor enlightened, and a flower is just a f lower:

> and yet, I'm here
> still hovering with
> aphids and marigolds.

She will soon revert to anger and anguish and in *Standing Here 2* feels "empty" as she empties her apron of rocks, the very birds upbraiding her: 'The robin overhead sings /I hear, "Your life is pure vanity."'

She seeks consolation from a Buddhist prayer for the reverence of all life, expressing the full joy and laughter about the "infinite love" all beings have for each other, but she is still not resigned, and in the next poem, *Entering the Holidays*, she vents her bitter grief of having to dress up and pretend things are okay when in fact she can't wait to leave "the toxic gathering" and return to a solitude that seems full of love, but we see is only inner and personal.

Towards the end of the elegy, she strings together five poems featuring flowers, the revival of the counter-metaphor to the entrapping labyrinth in the first poem. We have the listing of many flowers in *A Garden Full (II)*, which is often the turning point of a formal elegy, like the adornment of life and death and the coffin with the promise of beautiful revival, as with Whitman's lilacs. In *Planting Daffodils*, a friend's gift of these bulbs marks a turning point in relations with others, getting outside herself as she understands that "Our parallels run deeper than the soil. / I tuck these sweet daffodils in."

In the final poem, *Scattering Sweet Peas*, she recollects Natalie bringing in bouquets of them, but later the poet "alone" will leave a particular one, "the one in a million," a sign of her daughter, renewing in the garden. The elegiac progress is complete as Natalie resurfaces as a living thing that prevents the poet feeling divided from her daughter. Those sweet peas that announced their significance at the end of the first poem now finally become the resolving symbol of both impermanence and renewal.

This contemporary, very personal elegy shares the structure, themes, and symbols of a traditional elegy while employing familiar language and often colloquial phrasing to convey domestic scenes of joy and anguish. Ratnavira thereby ennobles the form and establishes for *Grief's Labyrinth* a place in a revered tradition.

ROBERT LOUIS CHIANESE, Ph.D. is Emeritus Professor of English at CSU-Northridge. A Fulbright Senior Specialist and the 1979 Mitchell Sustainability Laureate, he is a Past President, AAAS-PD and a columnist for *American Scientist* magazine.

islandviewmedia.com

Other Poems

Sometimes

Sometimes, love gives life
and with life's sweet breath
comes a joy so full
the heart cannot contain it.
Sometimes, life gives love
and with love's gentle truth
comes a happiness so full
death cannot extinguish it.

Ode to the Guardians of the Rain Forest

The trees here outnumber man,
powerful and protective.
They host his nourishment, his medicine,
the past, present and his future.
A living host to all,
they make known their presence with creaks and cracks
and crashing announcements.
In awe they stand yielding to rains and wind,
a beautiful strength man is too busy destroying
to comprehend.

From Her Sorrows

Even her daughter
turns her face
downward –
looking up again
with tears in her eyes
from whom the pain came
But even then
when the loving comes
bits of grace
and memories   long ago
covering the violence and drunken rages
into playing school   gardening
She smiles   good bye

"Excuse me,
do you know where I am going?"

How will I know when I get there?
How will I know when I am home?
I don't remember the address
the name of the street
but there was a yellow ribbon
around the oak tree in our front yard.
Baby song sparrows lived in the arches
and sometimes they fell.
Blue-bellied lizards waltzed on my fence.
Did you see the red-eared slider that rode our pool sweeper?
My mom painted his shell with her nail polish
so he wouldn't get lost.
Our dogs ate my coloring crayons,
pooped rainbows on the sidewalk
by the pond that would freeze over in the winter.
My brother cracked it with a screw driver
and told me to trust him.
Walk over it – "like Jesus."
I believed and fell.
I ate peanut butter and jelly sandwiches
shirtless on the patio.
I need to find it.
Will the new family let me see my room?
I remember Dad's leather chair
and mom's plaid chair.
I bet they are gone.
I saw a field where my brother and I
fed the horses carrots and sugar cubes.
If you could just help me find my way.
You see, I forgot my way home.

"Looking into Memories, Finding You Always There"

Whispering silently –
caution.
Loving without direction –
fear.
Where is the mystery
beyond purple mountains?
My unicorn has disappeared.

There's No Such Thing as Prince Charming

Sunshine
peeking through cobwebs
Castle walls deteriorating
Rain
seeping through the roof
Servants quarters flooded
Thunder
screaming through abandoned hallways
Echoes heard in the night
The princess
crying for what once was
Left
with broken dreams

Lovers Meet

And lovers glance
They purchase flowers on the street
They open up and take a chance
Then one is dead, their life complete
and the other learns
the red fern dance of mourning

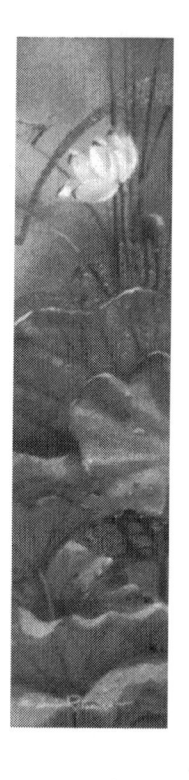

Once

A child gets
something in her head
it will never go away
no matter how many
tears she sheds
the memory will always stay

When Your Lover Dies

after MARGE PIERCY's *When A Friend Dies*

birds don't come to the feeder
travel brochures show you
what will be left uncharted
Nothing is earned by surviving
but survival
A famine depletes your will
for a dime in the fountain
A famine diminishes your hours
a waiting fills your minutes
and every customer at your table
leaves you empty for his face
When your lover dies
sleepless nights are no longer sated
mornings bring not hope
but a reawakening of a reality
that must be borne
When your lover dies
a touch is traded for a dream
sleep prevails   The heart fastens
A fire is unleashed
in your nightmares
that the dawn refuses to quench
At first consuming you
then inviting you
to the feeders
and the birds come back
as memories
and for a moment
you escape into joy

Representing Love

White satin trimmed with lace
representing innocence
The veil cascading down my face
representing mystery
excitedness and peace
My father and I
laughing, joking and talking
his reassuring presence
The *Wedding March* begins
his outstretched arm
representing strength
We walk together arm-in-arm
our last journey as only he and me
I belong no more to him only
We no longer are the same
I will be given a new name
yet I will always be his princess
and he my king
I am still flesh of his flesh and bone of his bone
It's a special father-daughter thing
yet now I journey with my prince
There's room enough to love them both
and one day I will give birth to my my own
representing both my prince and my king
and there will still be room to love
representing life and tradition

When a Son Is Born

The sidewalks amaze you with their complacency
After witnessing two sets of 10 and a victory cry
the man you have lain with
pales beside the beauty of his seed
Everything is altered by birthing
except birth
An expanse inflates your heart
for a dimple in the hand
A sense of purpose fills your seconds
nursing on demand
Every visitor leaves you wanting
time alone with your infant son
When a son is born
sleepless nights are now filled
with lullabies and intimacy
Mornings return you to one
as your love nourishes his kneading hunger
When pride and joy intertwine
joy wins, the heart opens
Then the joy births confidence
that possession can not hold back
At first it concerns you
then you honor independence
as this life begun within you
begins without you
and the child
like a memory
becomes sacred moments
of innocence

If Life Is a Snowflake

Each pain, each tragedy
is a scissor snip in the folds of our soul
creating a more
intricate design.
Pain has a purpose
each trial, a sliver of grace revealed
and for those of us who have lived
through so much pain and grief
we can take joy in knowing
God's scissors are taking extra time
in designing our unique formation
When we are complete
His love will create in us
a radiant beauty
shining for eternity

An Anthropomorphic Allusion

I like to imagine myself
        as an old gnarly oak tree
Others would ascribe to my knotty holes
        such attributes as wisdom and stature
to my serrated limbs
        perseverance and grace
Yes, I like to fashion the presence
        of its aged glory
far more than that of
        an inconsequential sapling
unable to withstand its first winter
snapping from the cold bite of its first squall

Rest with the Angels, Little One

We conceived you in love
We celebrated the
announcement of your arrival
We cherished our first glimpse of you
(on the ultrasound)
We created plans for you
We became concerned when
the pregnancy changed
You see, your sister's was not like this
We cried as the miracle of your life
was given to heaven above
cradled in the arms
of an angel to love

Ode to Sweet Peas

May their fragrance
dance into your doorways
May their beauty
behold your spirit
May their arrival
delight your visitors
And may your days
be filled with
their intoxicating
presence

First Kiss

Working side by side
in utter frustration I screamed,
"What do you want?!!"
The next moment I was enveloped
in his very being
his lips vibrating with an echo
inviting me to a
future
that mirrored my dreams.
It held promises
of the sounds of Africa,
adventures of
the Howler monkey's cries
in Panama,
the coral reefs unexplored
in Bermuda,
the Thor Hyerdall pyramid
in the Canary Islands,
the museums of
Madrid,
the Abaco Parrots in the Bahamas,
the Florida Keys
filled with snorkeling and
umbrella drinks.

Years later, on the beach with our mango margaritas
celebrating our anniversary barefoot,
he showers me with sapphires.
I thank God for dreams that come true
and that for once I let my soul listen.

Gamini

Each stroke
unhurried and researched
Each color
expertly chosen for depth and value
Each paintbrush
resembling the tools of eons
Each figure
reflecting triangles of light
Each sunbeam
catching the spirit of his laughter
Each raindrop
enveloping the pain of his sorrows
Each eye
reflecting the souls he has lived amongst
Each leaf
reflecting nature as it is full of lessons and wisdom
Each masterpiece, each signature
reflecting the beauty
that only his lifetime could create

When a Daughter Arrives

The day is witness to your trepidation
after observing her beauty
Your garden blooming with sweet peas
disperses its aroma
To glance at her tiny button of a nose
everything is altered by her arrival
except her smile
An awareness fills your heart
as she blesses you
with her angelic dimples
Visitors arriving with gifts of love
none that equal the gratitude
your family feels
now that she is home
as this dark haired beauty
possesses you with a joy
that births a love
woven with significance
Her arrival is your completion
and this life
begun without you
begins you
and this daughter
a mirage of promises
becomes the sacred moments
of your motherhood

My Husband's Touch

I admire his hands
painting the tropical birds
he has traveled over 50 countries to recreate
Awestruck by the images of Bo trees and feathers
they paint upon clayboard
Burnt sienna and sepia
collide into the earthen beauty
of his deeply etched hands
His Singhalese ardor touches
everything, awakening orchids
creating tropical rainforests
teeming with toucans and raucous macaws
caressing his canvases
with mist from the Amazon
I welcome his passions
Gamini's hands awaken
in simply brushing back my hair
etching my California paradigm
with his Sri Lankan touch

Today She Is 17

The year of my unfolding
It began with dreams, passion
and goals
that summer my fiancé Guy was killed
along with 16 other friends
and a part of me
became severed, too
Today she is 17
and I am 38
Without my loss
she would not be
my only daughter
Today is a brand new entrance
into a new life with new dreams
waiting to come forth
Today I bake cupcakes
and celebrate
and make a wish
for the young girl
I left behind

Mirrors

We are born loving them, trusting them
They are our first loves
our Alpha, our Omega
and all the letters in between
In time we judge more, love less
Disappointed with trust
we question
the foundations we grew upon
In loving others
our affection for
Oedipus and Electra
are replaced
They die loving us
trusting us
imploring forgiveness
From us   not for them
We are left with a legacy
for our children to explore
first teachers, first companions
each the other's reflection

inspired by *Faithless,* by Joyce Carol Oates
"For this is a fact I've learned that has surprised me a little: we come
to love our parents more as we grow older together, in a kind of
jolting lockstep. Realizing at the midpoint of our lives, looking at
them looking anxiously at us, My God, We're in this together."

My Father's Advice

My father once told me
the essential elements to life:
  become self-sufficient
  keep your word
  wake up and try again
  catch the moments of joy
  produce, think, grow
  learn, become humble
  be able to look in the mirror
    and be okay with what you see
    despite the world's opinion
  and that when all else is removed, trust remains
  to study a person's last five years
    as a likely pattern for the next five.

Based on all of these,
why should I hire you?

a leaf cutter ant colony most times exceed seven
million ants. In a twenty four hour work day
they harvest about
five tons of leaves

leaf cutter ants

Musical Faces

Our children want what they can't have
Our Sri Lankan American daughter
who looks like a petite Hawaiian dancer
wants to be a tall, buxom blonde-haired, blue-eyed diva
like the girls she played against in Sweden,
 where she placed second in the Gothia Cup.
Our 5'10"-tall, dark, handsome son
with a strong German build wrapped in ivory skin
wishes he were petite with almond eyes
to blend into the Japanese culture he is immersed in.
Our youngest son with blue-denim eyes and a dimpled chin
tans olive and flirts with his deep almond-shaped eyes
is studying Spanish, loves surfing in Mexico,
playing soccer and football with talented Hispanic teammates.
The music in his head must be salsa
as he wished for his sister's coloring so he can blend in.
Our children all want exactly what they were born without.
And we smile as they wish for what their friends possess
knowing one day the body they were born in
will be exactly what they were looking for –
the ones we so proudly show in our photographs
the souls we cherish in our hearts.

Hoping for Their Dreams

The gentleness of their hands
pouring for the first time
learning to hold the cup
pour the nutritious milk within
so hungry
three bowls of cream of wheat
two bowls of cereal
a banana and raisins
three cups of milk
and yet their tummies still hunger

How can two and three-year olds
eat this much
possibly 25 pounds
small as my sons on their first birthdays

I hunt the cupboards
find more to feed them
to fill them
their hungriness
calls to me

once a latch-key child
searching the cupboards
for food
so hungry
so yearning
so alone

We eat, we play
we read and dance
and make Play Doh shapes
We sift water and sand
we laugh
we scream
we touch

and when they awake frightened and crying
I hold them, sing them back to sleep
knowing their dreams are far too real
their lives far too filled with violence
too filled with a hunger their bodies do not yet own
their parents trying, working, applying
to gain a residence that is not half shelter-half drug rehab
and I believe they will make it

I have to
I have to hope beyond what I see
knowing by the age of four
they will have their vocabulary set
I introduce 1-12 in English, Spanish, American Sign Language
while we execute the dance steps of the Macarena

I am dancing them into more
The possibilities are endless
if only we can quiet their hunger pains
quiet their dreams
quiet the guns in their neighborhood

so the innocent can sleep and dream
of so much more than breakfast

Tipsy

She is adorning a tiara
tosses red velvet flower petals down the aisle
utters Russian nonsense to her auntie, the bride
blushing at her new uncle, the groom

She runs in circles during the ceremony
causing her older brother Nicholas much dismay
He chases her and returns her to her post

in the reception
her hair in ringlets, a very grown up up do
she downs her mama's champagne
running with the flute
smiles everywhere
enchanting us
with her pint sized appetite

Only three and a half years old
but she appears to be a happy gregarious drunk
She grabs her mama's camera
and instantly becomes a paparazzi
photographing mama, bride, self
and the Russian dancers
performing from the Bolshevik theatre

She claps   she skips
she sips champagne

her tiara slips
her head becomes heavy
eyelids too

This little Russian mini bride
whatever lies in your future –
your capacity for fun will sustain you

Today

I watched a towheaded angel
almost two
get taken away by two sheriffs
                and a Child Protective Service officer
Nothing we could do
Watched her strapped in and safely buckled
and removed to the nightmare of an unstable future
Our director applied for an emergency foster permit
Please god grant her that safe place

Today all the money in the world could not curb
the pain that echoed down our halls
Safe is a mirage
home is as intangible as ice
present then gone slipping away
like the memory of
being held
and then given away

Naptime

African lullabies permeate the room
rainsticks showering
the moment
darkness envelops, save one lit candelabra
as one caramel-kissed hand
reaches out to its alabaster mirror
thumbs entangle   fingers intertwine
comfort is found
hearts tremor   eyes flutter
sounds like heartbeats
echo with each caress
into the abyss
of innocence

I Will

I will wear crisp suits with starched collars
and shave twice a day
running strong hands over my chiseled jaw
lingering with scents of Drakkar Noir

I will waltz like a jaguar at night
after conquering the business world
During the daylight
I will arrive at my castle
with my children
running to welcome me
grab my wife in my arms and kiss her deeply
reminding her of the night to come

I will savor my home-cooked meal
sip my wine and broadcast my day to my family
remembering to inquire about homework
PTA meetings and charity events
I will relax in my recliner
while my domestic goddess
washes dishes and serves me dessert and coffee
massaging my Sampson-like shoulders

I will compliment her svelte figure and caress her hair
with tenderness – imagining the pleasures she will bring me
in my king-size bed

I will welcome her mouth upon mine
validating and accepting my very essence
and I will shower her with butterfly kisses
and gifts of such luxury no man could compare
and then my eyes will softly flutter
into dreams of contentment
as she attends to such matters as correspondence
bills and family birthday gifts
slipping into my arms afterwards
grateful to be so pampered

In the morning she will greet me with
coffee and the paper
and my pressed Italian suit will be
waiting in my wardrobe closet

I will entertain my reflection
with her admiring glances and
leave diamonds upon her pillowcase
You see, I am returning as the animus
you've never discovered

Speak to Me –

describe your ancestry
teach me your web of life giving symbiosis
sound out for me this breathtaking union
until I understand we are composed
of the same atoms
and both must live in beauty
before we become one
in our extinction

Learning the Rubik's Cube

As children we were taught to curl under our desks
when the bell rang – something about Russia and a Cold War.
We were quiet, we obeyed,
we longed to be outside.
It was the discovery of Pong and the Rubik's cube:
now the hiding under our desks made sense
if Russia did something, it was like
moving the red cube into the blue,
then we had to hide until it was all over.
I remembered the feeling of mastering my Rubik's cube
while listening to *Summer Nights* on my **Grease** 8-track.
Somehow, what one country does affects the other
the way green surrenders orange.
As an expectant mother, the father of my unborn child
was away at the Gulf War.
Somehow, what one country did affected my country
and the welcoming of a son
white evacuated red.
When he came home I took him to the VA hospital,
though he longed to be outside,
and raised our son on $7 an hour.
When he heard loud noises, he would duck,
the way we used to when the nuclear attack drill bell rang,
only it was no longer about Russia,
it was about Iraq and memories in this young father's head
orange invaded yellow.
And I recalled the way it felt
when, after days of twisting and turning
those 54 tiny cubes,
everything fell into place.
Only this time green wouldn't leave blue.

Dulce Et Decorum Est Pro Patria Mori

Gently she confessed to the young mother
echoing wisdom and grace,
"Love him as if there will not be another."
As she spoke a solitary tear caressed her face.
"Pray for and nourish this child
not only with the sweet nectar from your breasts,
but from the depths of your soul
for this period of unity lasts such a short while.
Soon he will take flight, leaving the sanctity of your nest.
My son, just 17, marched off to war.
I had raised him with the values of a Marine
to love this country he was now to fight for
and that was the death of my dream."
She grieved, for she had inadvertantly prepared
her precious lamb for an economic slaughter.
Now discerning why her son's life
was returned to his Creator,
she wept as she prayed for the children
of her daughter,
realizing his death was not for freedom
but the almighty dollar.
Quietly she cursed the times she had read to him
Horace's poetry:
        Sweet and becoming it is to die for one's country.

Returned Love

You loved me
You birthed me into this world of opportunity
and then gently placed me into the arms of another
where I was fed and cared for with others
and you provided for my financial desires
and we shared beautiful memories
during our quality time.

Many decades have passed
and I, in return, love you
and this world of opportunity we share.
I have carefully chosen your new home.
They will feed and care for you
and I will take care of your
financial requirements
and we will share beautiful moments
during the remainder of our quality time.

Women of Granite

Like ancient stones
we have directed
destiny's course.
Silently, stoically
standing firmly
we have founded and formed
every executive
each executioner
every Senator
each cell mate.
All owe their identity
to our wombs.
       As we enter
       this rapid movement
       with scars of silence
       we carry grace and wisdom
       into the echoing corridors
       and hurl the earth's core
       at the glass ceilings
       our ungrateful fetuses foolishly formed.

My Heritage

is linked to Celtic Boii
leaves me free to dance
to inhabit creativity
to defy social conventions
invites me
to pursue
music, color, love
a vagabond's passion
for people
for places, varied
in lieu of money
allows others
to disdain me
for my sense
of thievery
promiscuity
my inability
for permanence
a merry poverty
rooted in
letters of travel
granted by royalty
Perhaps
I inspire envy
in my
Bohemian
gypsy
revelry?

Tribute to My 60's Mother

I feel guilty about the ingratitude within me
I have to believe you tried to mark a path
Dying to get out of household tasks and
the mundane reality of day to day chores
you rallied your bra-burning sisters
and demonstrated with your signs held high
with unshaven armpits
Yes I have to believe you were trying
for indepenedence, freedom, and fair wages
If only you could see the predicament
you left your daughters in
our generation of Wonder Women
raised by career mothers
left inadequate to cook or mend
or even to take pride in our ability to give birth
Now we fight to do things just right
trying to achieve
perfection in two worlds
assertive career beauty by day
domestic goddess by night
The paradox is compelling
and I find myself hating you
more than my grandmother
who birthed 10 children
and whom I stand in awe of
idolizing her accomplishments
Yes I place my bra with nursing hooks on
and look in the mirror
hating the assertive career woman
who walks out on her infant each day
loving the grandma who taught me
how to cook and sing lullabies
Forgive my ingratitude, oh liberated woman
and love me now that you have the time to reflect
as I will one day love your granddaughter

I Say Hero

The young girls smile from ear to ear,
but the effervescence in their mama's smile
tells me he is home – he is safe,
survived kidnapping.
Torn from his family,
he has given up all of his worldly gain
to hire those who most would fear
 to return to his beloved's arms,
hold once more his loving children .
Home, back at work that same day, grateful,
his family once again whole.
Funny: those who share his color were his captors,
those who share his color – coyotes – were his rescuers.
Fair-skinned men of the upper classes
tore him from his beloved,
yet run from their own, hire their brothers
to allow them to abandon their mirror images, the women
they once vowed to love always, at an altar
in front of their Savior – their blue-eyed, fair-skinned Savior –
yet they too run.
Only their journeys are sanctioned,
allowed, even finance this deception.
Many call my hero "illegal, wetback, unwanted."
I say, "hero, lover of family, hard worker, beloved."
I say, "Give me 10 men like this
over one fair-skinned deceiver of children,
abandoner of wives,
of hidden incomes from secret accounts and alliances."
Funny how depending on the lens,
a hero is an illegal,
a fair-skinned corporate man the coyote.

Traveling with Pen and Brush

2001

Mother's Earth Montana
Sheets of rain
nourish the earth
Green trees restore
our spirits
Inhaling the very touch
of a mother's love

Silent Tears

Trickling so unassumingly beside the majestic 90-foot falls
pouring forth your gentle spirit
tirelessly forming
the firmness of the granite
while nourishing the ferns and lichens
to encompass a beauty
far beholding due to the powerful falls beside
the tender streamlets
pouring forth like an angel's tears
over lost memories

Marymere Falls, 1999

Bermuda, 2002

Waves lapping, pink coral
disguising secret worlds below
Boilers filled with parrot fish, sergeant majors, puffers,
sturgeons, wrasse, sea cucumbers, cow fish, brain coral and
dancing sea fans

Anticipating a mermaid to appear
one is lost
in this immersion of beauty and solitude

Emerging
one is enchanted
by pink houses with blue shutters
surrounded by shades of oleander and hibiscus
and white roof tops cleverly collecting every rain drop

The day is filled with ferry rides
shopping at Heritage House gallery and Triminghams
enjoying afternoon tea with friends
Refreshed, one slips away
from this Bermudaful day
into the symphony
of a million whistling tree frogs
lulling the island to sleep

Like a favored child
one is surrounded
by the love of this Island

Cape Buffaloes

Power in numbers

Entering Skukuza at dusk
a wash of chocolate hues
One of the most dangerous animals in Africa
peacefully munching on love grass
with a herd 100 strong
The curves of their horns
the strength of their bodies
Amazed we observed
      both their collective majesty
      and the power of their unity

African Elephants

Honoring the matriarch

Here in Letaba
the elephants bathe here
playfully dancing and rolling in mud
living these moments like gods worthy of pleasure
The herd of 40 is led
by a maternal love six decades strong
Their love and their grief
symbolize the pain and beauty
of Africa herself – a living legacy

African Bulls

Sacred friendship

Their ears lovingly recreate
the continent they adorn
The solitary males often bond
like the Askari tribesmen
An older bull shares the wisdom of survival
to the younger bull who returns
power and heightened senses for protection
This friendship is not based on blood, purely a kindness
Observations of stripped Mopani branches, fresh dung and urine
With 18x20-inch footprints
       and mud marked 8 to 10 feet high on a baobab tree
these signs let you know magic is approaching

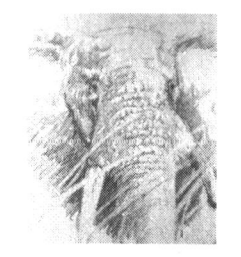

Rhino

A strength that is disappearing

Endangered and adorning a horn that others covet
thick skin like armor
collectively circles in protection
from a wayward young bull elephant
Warding off a danger
a wealthy banker will execute this devastation
for a momentary feeling of potency
Long eyelashes protect an old soul taking in his surroundings
Oxpeckers adorn him as ornaments of beauty
He disappears
      like an ace poker player
never showing his hand
leaving us with more questions than information to understand

Lion

The romance of the hunt

Out on an open jeep safari
two brothers – lips smacking grazed by my foot –
on the hunt of a warthog with foot long tusks
The power of teamwork
will increase their ability
to one day have a herd of lionesses to do their hunting
much more adeptly
They will live just 12 years
So little time for such a kingdom
A growing awareness of the need to reproduce
awakens the passion within my spirit
The survival instincts awaken your sensuality to a degree
that modern man has become numb
to African love grass, animals mating openly
remind one of the very reason we are alive
        Such passion for life
        must be returned to each of us merely surviving

Leopard

The agility of the hunter

In Mala Mala
the leopard's survival skills were observed
A kill, an impala, two-thirds of its size
dragged up in a tree – for safe keeping
Power and agility without
survival knowledge is worthless
The wisdom of the leopard – priceless

Refuge of Regeneration

African Baobab, *Adansonia digitata,*
in silent dominion, oversees sun-burnt plains,
nourishes myriad life cycles, comforts
the spiritual thirst of those seeking refuge,
capable of water storage,
offering dens to live and die in,
a place of spiritual intensity –
home to snake, frog, scorpion,
bush baby, bat, bee.
These gnarled gray behemoths,
born before the birth of Christ,
baptize Transvaal tribal baby boys
in water blessed with bark, symbolizing
a mighty strength, an ability to provide shelter
for the future, when red-billed buffalo weavers
will build colonies of nests in branches clutching emptiness.

In myth, The Creator gifted her beauty to hyenas
who inadvertently planted her upside down
and have been laughing ever since.

Every 20 years, at midsummer's eve,
dozens of luminous white blossoms
with purple stamens appear.
pollinated by bats and bush babies.
Within hours, the blossoms drift down silently.
Seed pods -- oblong, hairy and covered with green
the texture of suede -- provide a feast,
soon dispersed by baboons, monkeys, antelope.
Elephants, endangered by captivity in Preserves,
strip the generative bark away from these icons,
gray gnarled giants of giving,
so forthright and obvious, hide
environmental complexities, cultural capacities:
living monuments to a continent.

Panamanian Poetry

Here when the rain begins
the winds chime in
and the tropical breezes
entice you
The warmth soothes
your hurried soul
reminding you to drink in
all of its wonder
as well as the water you taste
as it quenches you
The sounds of birds calling
and trees dancing
caress you like a lullaby
Yes, Panama is the kind of place
that will inspire the weary
and heal the pain
of our hurried pursuit
in a way that leaves one understanding
the interconnectedness of all life forms
is in the essence of the rain forest

Trinidad Poems

Bamboo encounter
blue crowns, Racket-tails seeking
solace in the shade

    Stream frogs announce with
    bright yellow throats rain is here
    Mating in such bliss

Morpho butterfly
emerging after the rain
undulating grace

    Imaginary
    night walk   ocelot and snakes
    laughing with the bats

Harold's girlfriend ate
rice, beans, fruit and vegetables
Her cancer is gone

    A thought searches me
    I find it in my dreaming
    my grandmother's poem
    Decades later I
    touch her face in a photo
    Her laughter echoes mine

Searching For

A fisherman's net –
ties and knots, unraveling
yet sustaining life
through its snare
depending if your soul is
clothed in skin, feathers or scale.
It is foe or friend.
The gentle hands that free the fish
expertly carve and fillet
intricately tie and weave
feeding the pelican
that hovers nearby
perhaps contemplating if the Sa-skya Monastery
still searches these 60+ years
for the one pursuing small acts of kindness
patience, fortitude
and the capacity to remain
silent and alone for hours
in order to provide
for the loved ones he leaves behind each dawn.
This same painstaking observation
mending, tendency to breathe
deeply and quietly
ties and binds and sustains
those lucky enough
to take shelter with him
those who eat at his table
share his sea-weathered smile.
Do they wonder perhaps if this
is the 145th reincarnation of the Haiho Lama?
Or do they take for granted this seaworthy father
eating fish with his family
once again?

Snake Charmer

Teenage boys and gypsy men
make their living
fondling venom.
Cobras in baskets
unsheathe, undulate.
Pythons unyield, unfold
against their bodies.
Russell's vipers escape basket tops.
Fear requires payment.
Flutes awaken this
awareness of Eve
and for 200 rupees, he will leave.

Tsunami

Water without warning
Laughter lost, love lingering
The yin – tragedy
Motherless daughters
sonless fathers
The yang – a glimpse of world peace
Generosity without agenda
gratitude without grudges
Universal healing evident
in a borderless mourning

Sigiriya Fortress

5th Century *(477-495 AD)*

Striding along water and rock gardens
imagining King Kashyapa in all his glory.
1,800 steps to his outcrop,
with auditoriums, pools, a throne cooled with water
and advanced archeology
seeming to absorb his sense
of power, his ill-wrought crown.
And yet his brother, in just one quest
to revenge his father's murder, failed.
Perhaps King Kashyapa was preordained
to be king, destined to build
this very place, ringing with
contemplation and creation,
echoing with the songs, tempestuous liaisons,
the strategies birthed here.
Today it is the second greatest attraction for tourism –
only the elephants preceed it
– a singular reminder of second choice, of a son
lacking entitlement, earning the respect
of generations, of centuries to come and pay homage
to the power of defeating caste
with ambition.

Sanctuary

A child approaches
waters the sacred Bo tree seven times.
Seven wishes, seven pledges, seven promises to awaken.

Alighting the nearest branch, a Paradise flycatcher
looks upon this child
with the tenderness of a Buddhist monk.
The child's prayers surround
the trailing feathers of the flycatcher.
A monk's robes
donning a spiritual being
in the middle path widening to include
tree, bird and child
wrapped in the wishes
of innocence
blessed by the waters
of tranquilty.
The beauty of maroon orange
feathers, robes, sarong,
wrapped in unity
transformed and melded
into peace.

Ayuvedic Massage

I am greeted with *Ayubowan*
and enter my room.
My masseuse, Ruwani,
which means beautiful girl,
gestures for me to disrobe
and asks me where I am from.
Her smile lights the room
encourages my vulnerability.
She wraps me in a sarong
and massages my scalp
with sandalwood oil.
With care she begins
massaging away the aches and pains
from hiking Sigiriya's 1,800 steps.
My once tight calves resist then relax
beneath her strong and healing touch.
When she pops my toes I laugh.
When she notices my c-section scar
she shows her friend.
A rarity in their country.
Her compassion that my babies did not fit
is evident in the gentle undulations
upon my belly. I relax
releasing my insecurities
into the surety of her kindness.
Her massage of arms, legs, breasts,
buttocks, is healing
with a touch so confidant
so caring, years melt away
as I am touched once again
as an infant in the tub
sheer joy, fears yet unknown.
Sighing with satisfaction
I am led by hand
into the sauna with leaves and charcoal
melting away toxins.
I meditate on *Ayubown:*
"may all beings live long."

Her smile arrives and she leads
me to a steam chamber.
Water and coals, my body enclosed
and she massages my face
with avocado cream
then gently places the sheet over my face
for a steam.
Again thoughts of dreaming.
Moments of gratitude enter
as stresses depart and vaporize
the last moments of redress
and bowing to *Ayubowan* are
lovingly served and satiated
with 25 herbs in my tea.
I am convinced I am dreaming,
extend my gratitude
with the 1,700 rupees. An awareness
of healing, of a self image
lacking the kindness of a mother's touch
and I exit a woman capable of childbearing
of nursing, of accepting this vessel
I am awakening within.

Sri Lanka

Resplendent Isle
filled with rice and tea
smiles for everyone
women with beautifully colored saris
sweeping early mornings
children adorned in crisp, bright white kits
on their way to temple, to mosque,
to church, to school
Singhalese Buddhists amidst Burghers, Tamils,
Gypsies, Veddhas, Malays and Moors
all working, all surviving
despite the ravages of war and damages of a tsunami
People pray for peace
Mythology and superstition permeate
a variety of faiths and beliefs
arranged marriages and partnerships
built on love and passion
coexist side by side
Elephants, second only to man,
work and display majesty as one,
bathing in rivers, rolling in mud,
tending to young, yearning to mate,
somehow at times preceding man
in living these singular moments
Strong wiry men bare-bodied in sarongs
working hard, playing cricket and football,
romancing beautiful women
and still there is time to toast with friends
This moment
this island
this belief
in man and beast
co-existing in respectful harmony

Waking Up in Colombo

Fisherman casting his net,
spot-billed pelican waiting for charity,
grey heron near lotus flowers,
water monitor on a log,
women in saris, like butterflies,
children in white school uniforms,
fathers in sarongs and pressed shirts,
Muslim prayers over a loud speaker,
Hindu bells,
Buddhist chants echoing,
rosary beads kneading,
the sweet crisp crepe and soft yolk of an egg hopper,
the aroma of spiced tropical earth from Ceylon tea:
waking –
like stepping through
an imaginary veil,
feeling paradise
before your awakening arrives.

To the Lady Sewing at Night in a Red Room

The sun has gone to sleep.
Your children are home from school,
chores done, dinner served
and now resting peacefully
tucked beneath a pink mosquito net.

You have cooked, swept, washed
their white uniforms in the river
ironed them, prepared their evening meal,
all in a beautiful sari
with your captivating smile
and long dark tresses cascading
your smooth sun-kissed skin.
I see you.
I have you deep in my subconscious.
I struggle with my definitions
of femininity, of a woman's role
and I drink you in with my eyes,
with my heart.
You are the mother I dreamt of.
You are the mother I aspire to become.
My children – loved and healthy –
have a mother who works while they are in school.
I hear of European men, struggling
with powerful, accomplished women,
tired of empty homes and cold unmade beds,
coming to your village, choosing a Singhalese girl to wed,
uprooting her from this tropical, spice-laden island.
In her isolation, she withers and fades.
You are still stitching,
earning extra money for your family,
filled with your communal definition
of being the lady of the house.

Your womb fulfilled,
your breasts touched and suckled
your hair long and brushed
your wrist adorned with string,
a symbol of wakefulness,
your eyes content with loving.
Oh beautiful, Rashmi,
with every colored silk you stitch
memories of love,
of holding your loved ones,
guide your experienced hands,
encourage your steadfastness.
For you, men are not your competitor.
They are your protector, your provider.
Your role since the Fifth Century BC
is one of honor.
What can I bring to our 200-year history?
How can I bridge this ethereal beauty
with our barren progress?
I feel your beauty, your strength,
your creativity
in that red earth room.
I salute you. I celebrate you.
I take you home
in the canyons of my being.

THANKS

To my loving family:

husband **Gamini**

sons **Beau, Brooks** and stepson **Neil** –
all of whom gave me the laughter, belief and hope
to keep writing through the pain of our grief.

my **parents** and **extended family** and **friends** –
for every meal, conversation, memory, gift in
Nat's honor, your infallible presence carried us
through many difficult times.

Thank you for your constant and loving presence in my life,
for your belief in my ability to name this and to try in my most
vulnerable way to reach out to others who grieve or who assist
those who sometimes get lost in the labyrinth of sorrow and of
reliving love – for that is the process of embracing loss.

•

Special thanks to **Bill Harding**, editor-in-chief and publisher,
and editors **Rae Rose** and **Penny Perry** for their hard work –
most of all for being my poetry family.

The Way People Grieve

I love the way people grieve
as deeply as they have loved,
released from the pressures
of how they look
or what the Jones' have been doing:
pushed to the edge,
no longer requiring
other people's approval.

I love
the one who goes to work and pays the bills,
focusing on the one thing still in her control,
the one who becomes a recluse,
unable to tell her story yet,
the one who paints or sculpts or gardens
his mourning into beauty.

I love the cracks around their eyes
and in their voices,
revealing the price of love.
This debt, despite its heart wrenching weight,
is worth those moments of joy,
so filled with beauty,
 it will take a lifetime to remember.

Lisa Ratnavira holds a Master's degree from Concordia University. She has traveled with her husband Gamini to Africa, Sri Lanka, Bermuda, Panama, Trinidad, Abaco, Singapore, Japan, and other exotic and beautiful locations, all of which have inspired Gamini's tropical wildlife artwork and Lisa's nature writing and her poetry.

With poems published in *Poet, Bereavement, San Diego Poetry Annual, Lucidity, Abbey Press, Sky Blue Waters, Limestone Circle, Poets Pen, Poets Fantasy Magazines.* Lisa's chapbooks include **Traveling with Pen and Brush** and **Maiden, Mother, Crone.**
(available at gaminiratnavira.com)

She and Gamini live in Fallbrook, California, along with three dogs, three cats, koi, aquariums, aviaries and are visited by over 90 different species of birds each year at their feeders.

They look forward to more traveling and to continuing the scholarships in their daughter Natalie's name.

email: lratnavira@yahoo.com

Gamini Ratnavira is an internationally renowned and sought-after bird, mammal and mineral artist.

He has illustrated *Mammals of Sri Lanka, Birds of Sri Lanka* and is currently working on a biography and on *Endemic Birds of Sri Lanka.*

His signature includes a dragonfly next to his name. Since June, 2012, he has added "Nat" to each painting he creates.

His art can be viewed at gaminiratnavira.com.

His dramatic painting of a Red-tailed Hawk appears on the cover of the *2016-17 San Diego Poetry Annual.* A companion piece, *Coyotes at Twilight*, appears on the back cover of the anthology.

He and wife Lisa reside in rural Southern California. Their gallery – **The Hidden Forest** – is filled with gardens, aviaries and art. Open to the public, the gallery is located at 936 S. Live Oak Park Road, Fallbrook, California 92028.   (760)-703-2927

CREDITS

Illustrations:

      p. 53: NATALIE RATNAVIRA

    all others: GAMINI RATNAVIRA

gaminiratnavira.com

ACKNOWLEDGMENTS

Some poems in this collection have been previously published.

San Diego Poetry Annual
2007: *To the Lady Sewing at Night in a Red Room*
2008: *Trinidad Poems*
2009-10: *From Her Sorrows*
2010-11: *"Excuse me, do you know where I am going?"*
2012-13: *The Mobile*
2013-14: *Learning to Release*
2014-15: *Searching For*
2015-16: *And Yet*
2016-17: *Scattering Sweet Peas*

Maiden, Mother, Crone: *Tribute to My 60's Mother*

Lucidity
Summer, 2011: *My Heritage*

Made in the USA
Middletown, DE
20 March 2021